the Yorkshire terrier

& Australian Silky terrier

A guide to selection, care, nutrition, upbringing, training, health, breeding, sports and play

Content

Foreword

The book you are holding in your hands right now is by no means a complete book about the Yorkshire and the Australian Silky terrier. If we had collected all the information about these breeds, their history and development, feeding, training, health, and whatever else there is to know, this book would have consisted of at least five hundred pages.

What we have done, however, is to bring together all the basic information that you as a (future) owner of a Yorkie or Silky need to know in order to handle your pet responsibly. Unfortunately, there are still people who buy a pet without thinking through what they are about to get into.

This book generally deals with the history of these terriers, the breed standards and the advantages and disadvantages of buying a terrier. It also contains essential information about feeding and about the very first steps in training your dog. Reproduction, day-to-day care, health and breed-specific ailments are also topics.

After having read this book, you can make a carefully considered decision to buy a Yorkie or Silky and to keep it as a pet in a responsible manner. We advise you, however, not to rely solely on this book. A well-reared and trained dog is more than just a dog. Invest therefore in a puppy training course or an obedience course. There are also plenty of excellent books that deal with certain aspects, for which we do not have the space in this small book.

About Pets

A Publication of About Pets.

Copyright © 2003

About Pets

co-publisher United Kingdom

Kingdom Books

PO9 5TL, England

ISBN 1852791993

First printed

September 2003

Second print

December 2004

Original title: *de Yorkshire terrier*

© 2005 Welzo Media Productions bv,

About Pets bv,

Warffum, the Netherlands

www.aboutpets.info

Photos:

Rob Doolaard, Rob Dekker,

Printed in China through Printworks Int. Ltd.

In general

The Yorkshire terrier is a small, longhaired toy dog, which is also called Yorkie by its fans. Its character is lively, intelligent, sometimes overconfident and very friendly. It is also alert when it feels that something is wrong.

The Australian Silky terrier has been developed from the Yorkshire terrier, which is why it is also dealt with in this book.

Origin of the Yorkshire terrier

The Yorkshire originates in Great Britain. In the past, it was a little bigger and heavier and was used for pest control, especially against rats. The breed developed in Leeds and Halifax at the beginning of the second half of the nineteenth century. It is not sure which breeds form the basis of the Yorkie. It is likely that Skye terriers and Maltesers were used, and probably also the Black and Tan terrier or Manchester terrier. Some people claim that the Dandie Dinmont was also used. The dogs were first bred for uniformity, and later on they were bred smaller and smaller. The weight, which used to be 5 to 6 kilos in the past, is now only 1 to 2.5 kilos. Besides these show-dwarfs, there are of course still some bigger individuals.

Origin of the Australian Silky terrier

The Australian Silky terrier, which used to be called Sydney Silky or Silky Toy terrier in the past, was first bred in Australia at the end of the 19th century. The breed combines the best characteristics of both the Australian terrier and the Yorkshire terrier, which was imported around the turn of the century. In 1872, the first blue and tan Silky terrier participated at an Australian dog show.

These dogs were eventually imported to England and probably crossed with Clydesdale terriers to improve the coat structure. This small breed was never developed to serve man as pest control, but was bred purely as a companion. These active, inquisitive terriers have a more luxurious coat than the Yorkies. They are lightly built, compact dogs, which have fairly short legs. They can have both upright and hanging ears, but only the dogs with upright ears appear at dog shows.

Breed standard

A standard has been developed for all breeds recognised by the FCI (Fédération Cynologique Internationale). The FCI is the umbrella organisation of the Western European dog world. The officially approved breed associations of the member countries provide translations of the breed standard. This standard provides a guideline for breeders and inspectors. It is something of an ideal that dogs of each breed must strive to match. With some breeds, dogs are already being bred that match the ideal. Other breeds have a long way to go. There is a list of defects for each breed. These can be serious defects that disqualify the dog, in which case it will be excluded from breeding. Permitted defects are not serious, but do cost points in a show.

The Breed Standard of the Yorkshire Terrier

General Appearance

Long-coated, coat hanging quite straight and evenly down each side, a parting extending from nose to end of tail. Very compact and neat, carriage very upright conveying an important air. General outline conveying impression of vigorous and well proportioned body.

Silky terrier

Characteristics

Alert, intelligent toy terrier.

Temperament

Spirited with even disposition.

Head and Skull

Rather small and flat, not too prominent or round in skull, nor too long in muzzle; black nose.

Eyes

Medium, dark, sparkling, with sharp intelligent expression and placed to look directly forward. Not prominent. Edge of eyelids dark.

Yorkshire terrier

Ears

Small, V-shaped, carried erect, not too far apart, covered with short hair, colour very deep, rich tan.

Mouth

Perfect, regular and complete scissor bite, i.e. upper teeth closely overlapping lower teeth and set square to the jaws. Teeth well placed with even jaws.

Yorkshire terrier

Neck
Good reach.

Forequarters
Well laid shoulders, legs straight, well covered with hair of rich golden tan a few shades lighter at ends than at roots, not extending higher on forelegs than elbow.

Body
Compact with moderate spring of rib, good loin. Level back.

Hindquarters
Legs quite straight when viewed from behind, moderate turn of stifle. Well covered with hair of rich golden tan a few shades lighter at ends than at roots, not extending higher on hindlegs than stifles.

Tail
Customarily docked
Docked: Medium length with plenty of hair, darker blue in colour than rest of body, especially at end of tail. Carried a little higher than level of back. Undocked: Plenty of hair, darker blue in colour than rest of body, especially at end of tail. Carried a little higher than level of back. As straight as possible. Length to give a well balanced appearance.

Gait/Movement
Free with drive; straight action front and behind, retaining level topline.

Coat
Hair on body moderately long, perfectly straight (not wavy), glossy; fine silky texture, not woolly. Fall on head long, rich golden tan, deeper in colour at sides of head, about ear roots and on muzzle where it should be very long. Tan on head not to extend on to neck, nor must any sooty or dark hair intermingle with any of tan.

Colour
Dark steel blue (not silver blue), extending from occiput to root of tail, never mingled with fawn, bronze or dark hairs. Hair on chest rich, bright tan. All tan hair darker at the roots than in middle, shading to still lighter at tips.

Size
Weight up to 3.2 kgs (7 lbs).

Faults
Any departure from the foregoing points should be considered a fault and the seriousness with which the fault should be regarded should be in exact proportion to its degree and its effect upon the health and welfare of the dog.

Note
Male animals should have two apparently normal testicles fully descended into the scrotum.

Courtesy of the Kennel Club UK, July 2001

The Breed Standard of the Australian Silky Terrier

General Appearance
Compact, moderately low-set, medium length with refined structure; sufficient substance to suggest ability to hunt and kill domestic rodents. Straight silky hair parted from nape of neck to root of tail, presenting a well-groomed appearance.

Characteristics
Terrier-like, keen, alert, active.

Temperament
Very friendly, quick and responsive.

Head and Skull
Moderate length, slightly shorter in length from tip of nose to between eyes than from there to top rear of occiput. Moderately broad between ears; skull flat, without fullness between eyes. Nose black.

Eyes
Small, round, dark as possible, not prominent, keen intelligent expression.

Ears
Small V-shaped, with fine leathers, high on skull and pricked; entirely free from long hair.

Mouth
Jaws strong, with a perfect, regular and complete scissor bite, i.e. upper teeth closely overlapping lower teeth and set square to the jaws. Teeth even and not cramped, lips tight and clean.

Neck
Medium length, refined, slightly arched. Well covering with long silky hair.

Silky terrier

Forequarters
Shoulders fine, well laid back, well angulated upper arms fitting snugly to ribs; elbows turn neither in nor out; forelegs straight with refined round bone, set well under body with no weakness in pasterns.

Body
Slightly longer than height. Level topline; well sprung ribs extending back to strong loins. Chest of moderate depth and breadth.

Hindquarters
Thighs well developed. Stifles well turned; when viewed from behind, the hocks well let down and parallel.

Feet
Small, well padded and cat-like. Closely knit toes with black or very dark toenails.

Tail
Customarily docked.
Docked: Carried erect; not over-gay. Free from long feathering.
Undocked: Carried erect, not over-gay. Free from long feathering. Length to give an overall well-balanced appearance.

Gait/Movement
Free, straight forward without slackness at shoulders or elbows. No turning sideways of feet or pasterns. Hindquarters have strong propelling power with ample flexibility at stifles and hocks. Viewed from behind, movement neither too close nor too wide.

Coat
Straight, fine and glossy; silky texture; length of coat 13-15 cms (5-6 ins) from behind ears to set-on of tail desirable. Legs, from knees and hocks to feet, free of long hair. Fine silky 'top-knot', not falling over eyes. Long fall of hair on foreface and cheeks undesirable.

Colour
Blue and tan, grey-blue and tan, the richer these colours the better. Blue on tail very dark.

Distribution of blue and tan as follows:
Silver-blue or fawn top-knot, tan around base of ears, muzzle and on side of cheeks; blue from base of skull to tip of tail, running down forelegs to near knees and down thighs to hocks; tan line showing down stifles, and tan from knees and hocks to toes and around vent. Blue colour must be established by 18 months of age.

Size
Most desirable weight about 4 kgs (8-10 lbs). Height approximately 23 cms (9 ins) at withers, bitches may be slightly less.

Faults
Any departure from the foregoing points should be considered a fault and the seriousness with which the fault should be regarded should be in exact proportion to its degree and its effect upon the health and welfare of the dog.

Note
Male animals should have two apparently normal testicles fully descended into the scrotum.

Courtesy of the Kennel Club UK, July 2001

Buying

Once you've made that properly considered decision to buy a dog, there are several options. Should it be a puppy, an adult dog, or even an older dog? Should it be a bitch or a male dog, a pedigree dog or a cross?

Are you looking for a companion or a real show dog? Of course, the question also comes up as to where to buy your dog. Are you going to buy it from a private person, a reliable breeder, or would you maybe even get it from an animal asylum? It is important for you and the animal that you sort out these things in advance. You want to find a dog that fits in with your situation.

With a puppy, you choose a playful, energetic housemate, which will adapt easily to its new surroundings. If you want something a little quieter, an older dog is a good choice.

Advantages and disadvantages

The long silky coat of these two breeds needs plenty of care every day. This can be both an advantage and a disadvantage. Some people do not enjoy spending a lot of time grooming their dog, whereas others particularly enjoy making their dog as beautiful as possible. A well cared for Yorkie or Silky will get everybody's attention.

Neither the Yorkie nor the Silky has an undercoat. That means that they do not have a moulting period, but they need to be trimmed once in a while. The lack of an undercoat also has the advantage that these dogs don't spread that 'wet-dog-smell' when they got wet. A disadvantage is that these dogs have problems keeping themselves warm and that they will need some extra protection when it gets cold (jacket).

These dogs are very small and they fit into any house. This is, of course, an advantage. They don't need very much exercise, but it is better for them if they build up a good condition. They also both have a true terrier character and thus need a consequent, honest upbringing. Both breeds are very focused on their master and love to be with him as much as possible. They will follow you around all day long. Both breeds become very old and fifteen years is no exception. Both visitors and the postman are announced with loud barking.

Male or female?

Whether you choose a male or a female puppy, or an adult dog or bitch, is an entirely personal decision. A male typically needs more leadership because he tends to be more dominant by nature. He will try to play boss over other dogs and, if he gets the chance, over people too. In the wild, the most dominant dog (or wolf) is always the leader of the pack. In many cases this is a male. A bitch is much more focussed on her master, as she sees him as the pack leader.

A puppy test is good for defining what kind of character a young dog will develop. During a test one usually sees that a dog is more dominant than a bitch.

Puppy ...

... or adult?

You can often quickly recognise the bossy, the adventurous and the cautious characters. So visit the litter a couple of times early on. Try to pick a puppy that suits your own personality. A dominant dog, for instance, needs a strong hand. It will often try to see how far it can go. You must regularly make it clear who's the boss, and that it must obey all the members of the family. If you want to visit shows with your new companion, then you should choose an adventurous type and not the most timid puppy from the nest.

When bitches are sexually mature, they will go into season. On average, a bitch is in season twice a year for about two or three weeks. This is the fertile period when she can become pregnant. Particularly in the second half of her season, she will want to go looking for a dog to mate with. A male dog will show more masculine traits once he is sexually mature. He will make sure other dogs know what territory is his by urinating as often as possible in as many places as he can. He will also be difficult to restrain if there's a bitch in season nearby. As far as normal care is concerned, there is little difference between a dog and a bitch.

Puppy or adult?

After you've made the decision for a male or a female, the next question comes up. Should it be a puppy or an adult dog? Your household circumstances usually play a major role here.

Of course, it's great having a sweet little puppy in the house, but bringing up a young dog costs a lot of time. In the first year of its life it learns more than during the rest of its life. This is the period when the foundations are laid for elementary matters, such as house-training, obedience and social behaviour. You must reckon with the fact that your puppy will keep you busy for a couple of hours a day, certainly in the first few months. You won't need so much time with a grown dog. It has already been brought up, but this doesn't mean it doesn't need correcting from time to time.

A puppy will no doubt leave a trail of destruction in its wake for the first few months. With a little luck, this will only cost you a number of rolls of wallpaper, some good shoes and a few socks. In the worst case you'll be left with some chewed furniture. Some puppies even manage to tear curtains from their rails. With good upbringing this 'vandalism' will quickly disappear, but you won't have to worry about this if you get an older dog.

The greatest advantage of a puppy, of course, is that you can bring it up your own way. And the

upbringing a dog gets (or doesn't get) is a major influence on its whole character. Finally, financial aspects may play a role in your decision. A puppy is generally (much) more expensive than an adult dog, not only in purchase price but also in 'maintenance'. A puppy needs to go to the vet's more often for the necessary vaccinations and check-ups.

Overall, bringing up a puppy costs a good deal of energy, time and money, but you have its upbringing in your own hands. An adult dog costs less money and time, but its character has already been formed. You should also try to find out about the background of an adult dog. Its previous owner may have formed its character in somewhat less positive ways.

Two dogs?

Having two or more dogs in the house is not just nice for us, but also for the animals themselves. Dogs get a lot of pleasure from company of their own kind. After all, they are pack animals.

If you're sure that you want two young dogs, it's best not to buy them at the same time. Bringing a

dog up and establishing the bond between dog and master takes time, and you need to give a lot of attention to your dog in this phase. Having two puppies in the house means you have to divide your attention between them. Apart from that, there's a danger that they will focus on one another rather than on their master. Buy the second pup when the first is (almost) an adult.

Two adult dogs can easily be brought into the home at the same time, as long as they are used to each other. If this in not the case, then they need to get used to each other first. It is best to let the dogs get acquainted with each other on neutral territory. You will thus not encounter the problem that one of them will try to guard the territory. On neutral ground, e.g. a friend's garden where neither dog has been before, both dogs will be basically equal. You can then take them home and let them sort out the hierarchy among themselves.

Do not interfere in any 'quarrels', however. This might be a human reaction, but for the dog that is higher in the hierarchy it is as if its position is threatened. It will only show more dominant behaviour, with all the nasty consequences this might have. Once the hierarchy has been sorted, most dogs will get along very well.

Getting a puppy when the first dog is somewhat older often has a positive effect on the older dog. The influence of the puppy almost seems to give it a second childhood. The older dog, if it's been well brought up, can help with the upbringing of the puppy. Dogs like to imitate each other's behaviour. Don't forget to give both dogs the same amount of attention. Take the puppy out alone at least once per day during the first eighteen months. Make sure the older dog has enough opportunity to get some peace and quiet. It won't always be able to keep up with the speed of such an enthusiastic youngster. A puppy also needs to have the breaks put on once in a while.

The combination of a male and a female needs special attention. It is best to take two dogs of the same sex, as this will prevent a lot of problems. Castration or sterilisation is, of course, an option, but it is a final one. You will never be able to breed with a castrated or sterilised animal. Castration and sterilisation also have a big influence on the hormone balance, which can even change the coat structure in a way that it will get tangled or matted more easily. Get all the information you need before taking such a step.

A dog and children

Dogs and children are a great combination. They can play together and get great pleasure out of each other's company. Moreover children need to learn how to handle living beings; they develop respect and a sense of responsibility by caring for a dog (or another pet).

However sweet a dog is, children must understand that it is an animal and not a toy. These small terriers are quite fragile. A dog isn't comfortable when it's being messed around with. So make it clear what a dog likes and what it doesn't. Look for ways the child can play with the dog, perhaps a game of hide-and-seek where the child hides and the dog has to find it. Even a simple tennis ball can give enormous pleasure. Children must learn to leave a dog in peace when it doesn't want to play any more. A Yorkie or Silky must also have its own place where it's not disturbed. Have children help with your dog's care as much as possible. A strong bond will be the result.

The arrival of a baby also means changes in the life of a dog. Before the birth you can help get the dog acquainted with the new situation. Let it sniff at the new things in the house and it will quickly accept them. When the baby has arrived, involve the dog as much as possible in day-by-day events, but make sure it gets plenty of attention too.

Never leave a dog alone with young children! Crawling infants sometimes make unexpected movements, which can easily frighten a dog. And infants are hugely curious, and may try to find out whether the tail is really fastened to the dog, or whether its eyes come out, just like they do with their cuddly toys. Yorkshire terriers and Silkies always remain dogs: they will defend themselves when they feel threatened.

Where to buy

There are various ways of acquiring a dog. The decision for a puppy or an adult dog will also define for the most part where you buy your dog.

If it's to be a puppy, then you need to find a breeder with a litter. If you choose a popular breed, such as the Yorkie or Silky, there is choice enough. But you may also face the problem that there are so many puppies on sale that have only been bred for profit's sake. You can see how many puppies are for sale by looking in the regional newspaper every Saturday. Some of these dogs have pedigrees, but many don't. Breeders often don't watch out for breed-specific illnesses and in-breeding; puppies are separated from their mother as fast as possible and are thus insufficiently socialised. Never buy a puppy that is too young, or whose mother you weren't able to see.

Fortunately there are also enough bona-fide breeders of Yorkshire terriers and Australian Silky terriers. Try to visit a number of breeders before you actually buy your puppy. Ask if the breeder is prepared to help you after you've bought your puppy, and to help you find solutions for any problems that may come up.

Finally, you must realise that a pedigree is nothing more or less than a proof of descent. The Kennel Club also issues pedigrees to the young of parents that suffer from congenital conditions, or that have never been checked for these. A pedigree says nothing about the health of the parent dogs.

What to watch out for

Buying a puppy is no simple matter. You must pay attention to the following:

- Never buy a puppy on impulse, even if it is love at first sight. A dog is a living being that will need a lot of care and attention over a long period (for more than ten years). It is not a toy that you can put away when you're done with it.
- Take a good look at the mother. Is she calm, nervous, aggressive, well cared-for or neglected? The behaviour and condition of the mother is not only a sign of the quality of the breeder, but also of the puppy you're about to buy.
- Avoid buying a puppy whose mother has been kept only in a kennel. A young dog needs as many different impressions as possible in its first few months, including living in a family group. It gets used to people and possibly other pets. Kennel dogs miss these experiences and are inadequately socialised.
- Always ask to see the parents' papers (vaccination certificates, pedigrees, official health examination certificates).
- Let the breeder know if you have show ambitions with your future dog.
- Never buy a puppy younger than eight weeks.
- Put all agreements with the breeder in writing. A model agreement is available from the breed association.

Travelling with your Yorkie or Silk

There are a few things to think about before travelling with your dog. While one dog may enjoy travelling, another may hate it. While you might enjoy going on holidays to far-away places, it is questionable whether your dog does, too.

That very first trip

The first trip of a puppy's life is also the most nerve-wrecking. This is the trip from the breeder's to its new home.

If possible, pick up your puppy in the morning. It then has the whole day to get used to the new situation. Ask the breeder not to feed the puppy that day. The young animal will be overwhelmed by all kinds of new experiences. Firstly, it's away from its mother; it's in a small room (the car) with all its different smells, noises and strange people. So there's a big chance that the puppy will be carsick this first time, with the annoying consequence that it will remember travelling in the car as an unpleasant experience.

So it's important to make this first trip as pleasant as possible. When picking up your puppy, always take someone with you who can sit in the back seat with the puppy on his or her lap and talk to it calmly. If it's too warm for the puppy, a place on the floor at the feet of your companion is ideal. The pup will lie there relatively quietly and may even take a nap. Ask the breeder for a cloth or something else from its nest, which carries a familiar scent. The puppy can lie on this in the car, and it will also help if it feels lonely during the first nights at home.

If the trip home is a long one, then stop for a break (once in a while). Let your puppy roam and sniff around (on the lead!), have a little drink and, if necessary, let it do its business. Do take care to lay an old towel in the car. It can happen that the puppy, in its nervousness, may urinate or be sick.

It's also good advice to give a puppy positive experiences with car journeys as soon as possible. Make short trips to nice places where you can walk and play with it. It can be a real nuisance if your dog doesn't like travelling in a car. You will always come across situations when your dog needs to travel in the car, such as when taking it to the vet's or to visit friends.

Taking your dog on holiday

When making holiday plans, you also need to think about what you're going to do with your dog during that time. Are you taking it with you, putting it into kennels or leaving it with friends? In any event there are a number of things you need to do in good time.

If you want to take your dog with you, you need to be sure in advance that it will be welcome at your holiday home, and what the rules there are. If you're going abroad it will need certain vaccinations and a health certificate, which normally need to be done four weeks before departure. You must also be sure that you've made all the arrangements necessary to bring

your dog back home to the UK, without it needing to go into quarantine under the rabies regulations. Your vet can give you the most recent information. If your trip is to southern Europe, ask for a treatment against ticks (you can read more about this in the Parasites chapter).

Although dog-owners usually enjoy taking their dog on holiday, you must seriously ask yourself whether the dog feels that way too. Yorkies and Silkies certainly don't always feel comfortable in a hot country. Days spent travelling in a car are also often not their preference, and some dogs suffer badly from carsickness. There are good medicines for this, but it's questionable whether you're doing your dog a favour with them.

If you do decide to take it with you, make regular stops at safe places during your journey, so that your dog can have a good run.

Take plenty of fresh drinking water with you, as well as enough of the food your dog is used to. Don't leave your dog in the car standing in the sun. It can quickly be overcome by the heat, which can have fatal consequences. If you really can't avoid it, park the car in the shade as far as possible and leave a window cracked for some fresh air. Even if you have taken all these precautionary measures: Don't stay away long!

If you're travelling by plane or ship, make sure in good time that your dog can travel with you and what rules you need to observe. You will need some time to make all the arrangements.

Maybe you decide not to take your dog with you, and you then need to find somewhere for it to stay. Arrangements for a place in kennels need to be made well in advance. There will be certain vaccinations required, which need to be given a minimum of one month before the stay. If your dog can't be accommodated in the homes of relatives or friends, it might be possible to have an acquaintance stay in your house. This also needs to be arranged well in advance, as it may be difficult to find someone who can do this. Always ensure that your dog can be traced should it run away or get lost while on holiday. A little tube with your address, or a tag with home and holiday

address, can avoid a lot of problems.

Moving home

Dogs generally become more attached to humans than to the house they live in. Moving home is usually not a problem for them. But it can be useful to let the dog get to know its new home and the area around it before moving.

If you can, leave your dog somewhere else (with relatives, friends, or in kennels) on the day of the move. The chance of it running away or getting lost is then practically non-existent. Once you have completed your move, you can pick your dog up and let it quietly get familiar with its new home and environment.

Give it its own place in the house at once and it will quickly adapt. During the first week or so, always walk your dog on a lead, because an animal can get lost in new surroundings too. Always take a different route so it quickly gets to know the neighbourhood.

Don't forget to get your new address and phone number engraved on your dog's tag. Send a change of address notice to the institution that has any chip or tattoo data. Dogs must sometimes be registered in a new community (just as people), and you must pay for a dog licence. In some communities, you get part of your fee back if you move within the year you paid for.

Feeding your dog

A dog will actually eat a lot more than just meat. In the wild it would eat its prey complete with skin and fur, including the bones, stomach, and the innards with their semi-digested vegetable material.

In this way the dog supplements its meat menu with the vitamins and minerals it needs. This is also the basis for feeding a domestic dog.

Ready-made foods
It's not easy for a layman to put together a complete menu for a dog, including all the necessary proteins, fats, vitamins and minerals in just the right proportions and quantities. Meat alone is certainly not a complete meal for a dog, as it contains too little calcium. A continuous calcium deficiency will lead to bone defects, and for a fast-growing puppy this can lead to serious skeletal deformities. If you put its food together yourself, you can easily give your dog too much in terms of vitamins and minerals,

which can also be bad for your dog's health.

You can avoid these problems by giving it ready-made food of a good brand. These products are well balanced and contain everything your dog needs. Supplements, such as vitamin preparations, are superfluous. The amount of food your dog needs depends on its weight and activity level. You can find guidelines on the packaging. Split the food into two meals per day if possible, and always ensure that there's a dish of fresh drinking water next to its food.

Give your dog the time to digest its food and don't let it outside straight after a meal. A dog should never play on a full stomach. This can cause stomach torsion (the stomach turning over), which can be fatal for your dog.

Because the food needs of a dog depend, among other things, on its age and way of life, there are many different types of dog food available. There are "light" foods for less active dogs, "energy" foods for working dogs and "senior" foods for the older dog. There is also special food for smaller dog breeds such as the Yorkie and the Silky. The manufacturers have taken the size of a miniature dog's muzzle into consideration when designing these feeds. The bits are somewhat smaller and the food is concentrated, so that miniature breeds receive all the necessary nutrients. The smaller packaging also prevents the food turning bad.

Canned foods, mixers and dry foods

Ready-made foods, which are available at pet shops or in the supermarket, can roughly be split into canned food, mixer and dry food. Whichever form you choose, ensure that it's a complete food with all the necessary nutrients. You can see this on the packaging.

Most dogs love canned food. Although the better brands are composed well, they do have one disadvantage: they are soft. A dog fed only on canned food will sooner or later have problems with its teeth (plaque, paradontosis). Besides canned food, give your dog hard foods or dog chews at certain times. Mixer is a food consisting of chunks, dried vegetables and grains. Almost all the moisture has been extracted. The advantages of mixer are that it is light and keeps well. You add a certain amount of water and the meal is ready. A disadvantage is that it must definitely not be fed without water. Without the extra fluid, mixer will absorb the fluids present in the stomach, which can cause serious problems. Should your dog manage to get at the bag and enjoy its contents, you must immediately give it plenty to drink.

Dry foods have also had moisture extracted, but not as much as mixer. The advantage of dry foods is that they are hard, forcing the dog to use its jaws, removing plaque and massaging the gums.

Dog chew products

Naturally, once in a while you want to spoil your dog with something extra. Don't give it pieces of cheese or sausage as these contain too much salt and fat. There are various products available that a dog will find delicious and which are also healthy, especially for its teeth. You'll find a large range of varying quality in the pet shop.

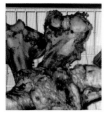

Smoked bones

Buffalo hide chews

The butcher's left-overs

The bones of slaughtered animals have traditionally been given to the dog, and dogs are crazy about them, but they are not without risks. Pork and poultry bones are too weak. They can splinter and cause serious injury to the intestines. Beef bones are more suitable, but they must first be cooked to kill off dangerous bacteria. Pet shops carry a range of smoked, cooked and dried abattoir residue, such as pigs' ears, bull penis, tripe sticks, oxtails, gullet, dried muscle meat, and hoof chews. Due to its size, the butcher's leftovers are often not suitable for small dog breeds such as the Yorkshire terrier and the Silky terrier.

Fresh meat

If you do want to give your dog fresh meat occasionally, never give it raw, but always boiled or roasted. Raw (or not fully cooked) pork or chicken can contain life-threatening bacteria. Chicken can be contaminated by the notorious salmonella bacteria, while pork can carry the Aujeszky virus. This disease is incurable and will quickly lead to your pet's death.

Cowhide and buffalo hide chews

Dog chews are usually made of cowhide or buffalo hide. The hide is knotted and pressed into chews. Your dog can enjoy a wide variety of chews, including shoes, twisted sticks, lollies and balls. They are nice to look at and a pleasant change. Make sure that the chews you buy are suitable for small dogs.

Munchie sticks

Munchie sticks are green, yellow, red or brown coloured sticks of various thicknesses. They consist of ground buffalo hide with a number of often undefined additives. Dogs usually love them because these sticks have been dipped in the blood of slaughtered animals. The composition and quality of these between-meal treats is not always clear. Some are fine, but there have also been sticks found, which contained high levels of cardboard and even paint residues. Choose a product whose ingredients are clearly labelled. The disadvantage of some of these sticks is that they can discolour the hair around the muzzle. They are thus less suitable for show dogs.

Overweight?

Recent investigations have shown that many dogs are overweight. A dog usually becomes too fat because of over-feeding and lack of exercise. Use of medicines, or a disease, is rarely the cause. Dogs that become too fat are often given too much food or too many treats between meals. Gluttony or boredom can also be a cause, and a dog often puts on weight following castration or sterilisation. Due to changes in hormone levels it becomes less active and consumes

less energy. Finally, simply too little exercise alone can lead to a dog becoming overweight.

You can use the following rule of thumb to check whether your dog is overweight: you should be able to feel its ribs, but not see them. If you can't feel its ribs then your dog is much too fat. Overweight dogs live a passive life, they play too little and tire quickly. They also suffer from all kinds of medical problems (problems in joints and heart conditions). They usually die younger too.

So it's important to make sure that your dog doesn't become too fat. Always follow the guidelines on food packaging. Adapt them if your dog is less active or gets lots of snacks. Try to make sure your dog gets plenty of exercise by playing and running with it as much as you can. If your dog starts to show signs of putting on weight, you can switch to a low-calorie food. If it's really too fat and reducing its food quantity doesn't help, then a special diet is the only solution.

Munchie sticks

Caring for your Yorkie or Silky

Good (daily) care is very important for your Yorkie or Silky. A well cared for dog is far less at risk of becoming ill. Looking after your dog is not just a necessity, but also a pleasure: master and dog give each other all their attention. It is also a great moment for a game or a cuddle.

The coat

Yorkshire puppies are born with a short coat. The longer hairs develop slowly. The steel-blue colour is still black on puppies, but they already display the tan markings. At the age of approximately three to six months, the colour changes from black to steel-blue, but it can happen as late as at twelve to eighteen months. At the age of two to three years, the coat has its final colour. The colour change starts on the head, which lightens up to a slate-blue and finally gets its end-colour. If your puppies are the right colour too early, they will probably become too light over time. Silky terriers are born completely black and with smooth hair.

Taking care of your dog's coat includes daily brushing or combing and checking for parasites (fleas). How often your dog needs to be brushed or combed depends on the length of the coat. You keep your Yorkie or Silky only as a companion and don't have much time for intensive grooming? Have your dog's coat trimmed at a grooming parlour. It is better to have a dog with a trimmed coat (although this is not really appropriate for the breed) than to have one with a tangled and matted coat.

Use the right equipment for your grooming sessions. Combs must not be too sharp, and choose a brush made of rubber or natural hair. Always brush or comb from the head to the tail and follow the direction of the hair. Carefully pluck tangles out with your finger, and don't pull them out. If you have a show dog, put curlers in its coat. You can also buy special curler paper from the breed association or at a grooming parlour. The curlers need to be taken out every day, then the coat needs to be brushed out very well before you reapply the curlers. If the curlers stay in for too long, painful tangles will develop.

If you get your puppy used to being brushed, bathed and blow-dried at a young age, it will learn to accept having its coat cared for. Only bathe your dog when it is absolutely necessary. Always use a special dog shampoo. It is best to wash Yorkies and Silkies with a shampoo based on mink oil. Make sure that no shampoo gets into the eyes and ears and wash out any suds well. Use a good dog conditioner after the shampoo. Carefully pat the dog dry with a towel after washing it. Don't rub it, as the wet hairs will easily break. Slowly blow-dry your dog. Set the hairdryer on the lowest setting and make plenty of circular movements, as the warm air can quickly become too hot. Only let your dog outdoors when it is completely dry, as dogs can catch colds too!

Your vet can prescribe special medicinal shampoos for some skin conditions. Always follow the

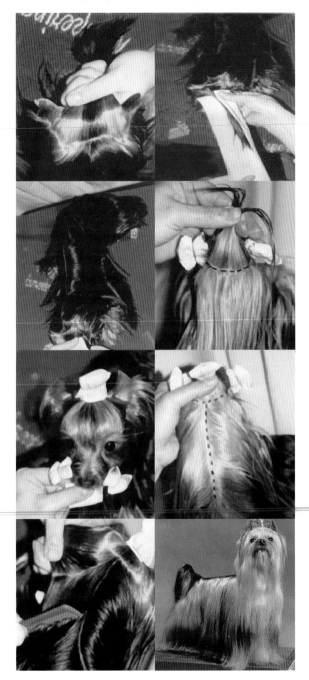

At the groomer's:
washing ...

drying ....

blow-drying...

combing

instructions. To prevent skin and coat problems, it is important to fight fleas well. Don't just treat the fleas on your dog, but also in its environment (see chapter Parasites). Coat problems can also be a result of an allergic reaction to certain feed ingredients. In these cases your vet will prescribe a hypoallergenic diet.

Teeth

A dog needs to be able to eat properly to stay in good condition. It thus needs healthy teeth. Regularly check your dog's teeth and molars. If you think that all is not well, contact your vet immediately. Regular feeds of hard dry food will help to keep your dog's teeth clean and healthy. You can buy special dog chews which prevent the formation of tartar and ensure a fresh breath.

The most effective way to care for your dog's teeth is to brush them. You can use a special dog toothbrush for this, but some gauze wrapped around your finger will also do the trick. If you get your dog used to having its teeth cleaned at an early age it will get used to it quite quickly. You can also get an older dog used to having its teeth cleaned. With a dog chew as a reward it certainly won't mind.

Nails

If your dog walks on hard ground a lot, its nails will normally wear down by themselves. If this is not the case, then you need to cut its nails. It will certainly not do any harm to check the length of the nails on a regular basis especially if your dog doesn't go out on the streets a lot. If you can push a paper between the ground and your dog's nail when it is standing, then it is the right length.

Nails that are too long can hinder your dog. It can injure itself when scratching. They therefore need to be cut. You can do this with special nail scissors from the pet shop. Be very careful not to cut the nail off too far, as you can easily cut into the quick, in which case it will bleed profusely. It is quite difficult to see where the quick begins in the nails of Yorkies and Silkies, because their nails have a dark colour. If you are unsure about cutting your dog's nails, let the vet or grooming parlour do it.

Eyes

You need to clean your dog's eyes every day. 'Sleepies' and bits of dried tear fluid can gather in the corners of the eyes. You can easily remove these by wiping downwards with your thumb. If you don't like doing this, use a bit of tissue paper.

At the groomer's:
looking like a hippy

Keeping your dog's eyes clean only takes a few seconds a day, so don't miss it! If the sleepies are yellow and slimy, then your dog will probably have a serious irritation or infection. You can usually solve this problem quite easily with eye drops, which you can get at your vet's. Prevent irritations by keeping the eyes clear of hair. You can do this by tying your dog's hair together with a bow on its head.

Ears

When looking after their dogs, many people forget the ears. They need to be checked at least once a week, though. If they are very dirty or contain a lot of wax, you will need to clean them. Do this preferably with a clean cotton cloth which you moistened with some warm water or baby oil. Don't use cotton wool because of the fluff it leaves behind. Never enter the ear canal with an object!

If the hair in the ears causes problems, it is best to remove it. Carefully pull it out between your thumb and index finger. If you neglect looking after your dog's ears, there's the risk of an ear infection. A dog that scratches its ears a lot might be suffering from dirty ears, and ear infection or ear mites. You will need to take it to the vet's as soon as possible.

Bringing up your terrier

It is very important that your dog is well brought up and obedient. It makes your dog's company not only more pleasant for you, but also for your environment.

A puppy can learn in a playful manner what it might do and what it must never do. Rewarding and being consistent are important tools when bringing up a dog. If you reward good behaviour with your voice, a cuddle or a treat, your dog will quickly learn to listen to you. A puppy training course can also help to show you the right way.

(Dis)obedience

A dog that won't obey you is not just a problem for you, but also for your surroundings. It's therefore important to avoid unwanted behaviour. In fact, this is what training your dog is all about, so get started early. Once again, 'Start 'em young!' should be your motto.

An untrained dog is not just a nuisance, but can also cause dangerous situations by running into the road, chasing joggers or jumping at people. A dog must be trained out of this undesirable behaviour as quickly as possible. The longer you let it go on, the more difficult it will become to correct. The best thing to do is to attend a special obedience course. This won't only help to correct the dog's behaviour, but its owner also learns how to handle undesirable behaviour at home. A dog must not only obey its master during training, but at home too.

Always be consistent when training good behaviour and correcting annoying behaviour. This means a dog may always behave in a certain way, or must never behave that way. Reward it for good behaviour and never punish it after the fact for any wrongdoing. If your dog finally comes after you've been calling it a long time, then reward it. If you're angry because you had to wait so long, it may feel it's actually being punished for coming. It will probably not obey at all next time for fear of punishment.

Try to take no notice of undesirable behaviour. Your dog will perceive your reaction (even a negative one) as a reward for this behaviour. If you need to correct your dog, then do this immediately. Use your voice or grip it by the scruff of its neck and push it to the ground. This is the way a mother dog calls her pups to order. Rewards for good behaviour are, by far, preferable to punishment; they always achieve a better result.

House-training

The very first training (and one of the most important) that a dog needs is house-training. The basis for good house-training is keeping a good eye on your puppy. If you pay attention, you will notice that it will sniff a long time and turn around a certain spot before doing its business there. Pick it up gently and place it outside, always at the same place. Reward it abundantly if it does its business there.

Another good moment for house-training is after eating or sleeping. A puppy often needs to do its business at these times. Let it relieve itself before playing with it, otherwise it will forget to do so and you'll not reach your goal. For the first few days, take your puppy out for a walk just after it's eaten or woken up. It will quickly learn the meaning, especially if it's rewarded with a dog biscuit for a successful attempt.

Of course, it's not always possible to go out after every snack or snooze. Lay newspapers at different spots in the house. Whenever the pup needs to do its business, place it on a newspaper. After some time it will start to look for a place itself. Then start to reduce the number of newspapers until there is just one left, at the front or back door. The puppy will learn to go to the door if it needs to relieve itself. Then you put it on the lead and go out with it. Finally you can remove the last newspaper. Your puppy is now house-trained.

One thing that certainly won't work is punishing an accident after the fact. A dog whose nose is rubbed in its urine or its droppings won't understand that at all. It will only get frightened of you. Rewarding works much better than punishment.

An indoor kennel or cage can be a good tool to help in house-training. A puppy won't foul its own nest, so a kennel can be a good solution for the night, or during periods in the day when you can't watch it. But a kennel must not become a prison where your dog is locked up day and night.

First exercises

The basic commands for an obedient dog are those for sit, lie down, come and stay. You can teach a pup to sit by holding a piece of dog biscuit above its nose and then slowly moving it backwards. The puppy's head will also move backwards until its hind legs slowly go down. At that moment you call 'Sit!'. After a few attempts, it will quickly know this nice game. Use the 'Sit!' command before you give your dog its food, put it on the lead, or before it's allowed to cross the street.

Teaching the command to lie down is similar. Instead of moving the piece of dog biscuit backwards, move it down vertically until your hand reaches the ground and then forwards. The dog will also move its forepaws forwards and lie down on its own. At that moment call 'Lie down!' or 'Lay!'. This command is useful when you want a dog to be quiet.

Two people are needed for the 'Come!' command. One holds the dog back while the other runs away. After about fifteen metres, he stops and enthusiastically calls 'Come!'. The other person now lets the dog free, and it should obey the command at once. Again you reward it abundantly. The 'Come!' command is useful in many situations and good for safety too.

A dog learns to stay from the sitting or lying position. While it's sitting or lying down, you call the command 'Stay!' and then step back one step. If the dog moves with you, quietly put it back in position, without displaying anger. If you do react angrily, you're actually punishing it for coming to you, and you'll only confuse your dog. It can't understand that coming is rewarded one time, and punished another. Once the dog stays nicely, reward it abundantly. Practise this exercise with increasing distances (at first no more than one metre). The 'Stay!' command is useful when getting out of the car.

Courses
Obedience courses to help you bring up your dog are available across the country. These courses are not just informative, but also fun for dog and master. With a puppy, you can begin with a puppy course. This is designed to provide the basic training. A puppy that has attended such a course has learned about all kinds of things that will confront it in later life: other dogs, humans, traffic and others. The puppy will also learn obedience and to follow a number of basic commands. Apart from all that, attention will be given to important subjects such as brushing, being alone, travelling in a car, and doing its business in the right places.

The next step after a puppy course is a course for young dogs. This course repeats the basic exercises

and ensures that the growing dog doesn't get into bad habits. After this, the dog can move on to an obedience course for full-grown dogs.

For more information on where to find courses in your area, contact your local kennel club. You can get its address from the Kennel Club of Great Britain in London. In some areas, the RSPCA organises obedience classes and your local branch may be able to give you information.

Play and toys

There are various ways to play with your dog. You can romp and run with it, but also play a number of games, such as retrieving, tug-of-war, hide-and-seek and catch. A dummy is ideal for retrieving, and you can play tug-of-war with an old sock or a special tugging rope. Start with tug-of-war only when your dog is a year old. A puppy must first get its second teeth and then they need several months to strengthen. There's a real chance of your dog's teeth becoming deformed if it starts playing tug-of-war too soon. You can use almost anything for a game of hide-and-seek. Never use too small a ball for games. It can easily get lodged into the dog's throat.

Play is extremely important. Not only does it strengthen the bond between dog and master, but it's also healthy for both. Make sure that you're the one that ends the game. Only stop when the dog has brought back the ball or frisbee, and make sure you always win the tug-of-war. This confirms your dominant position in the hierarchy. Use these toys only during play, so that the dog doesn't forget their significance.

When choosing a special dog toy, remember that dogs are hardly careful with them. So always buy toys of good quality, which a dog can't easily destroy. Be very careful with sticks and twigs. The latter, particularly, can easily splinter. A splinter of wood in your dog's throat or intestines can cause awful problems. Throwing sticks or twigs can also be dangerous. If they stick into the ground, a dog can easily run into them with an open mouth.

Aggression

Yorkshire and Australian Silky terriers are not normally aggressive. It can happen, however, that they are less friendly towards other animals or people. It is therefore good to know a bit more about aggressive behaviour in dogs.

There are two different types of aggressive behaviour in dogs: The anxious-aggressive dog and the dominant-aggressive dog. An anxious-aggressive dog can be recognised by its pulled-back ears and its lowly held tail. It will have pulled in its lips, baring its teeth. This dog is aggressive because it's very frightened and feels cornered. It would prefer to run away, but if it can't then it will bite to defend itself. It will grab its victim anywhere it can. The attack is usually brief and, as soon as the dog can see a way to escape, it's gone. In a confrontation with other dogs, it will normally turn out as the loser. It can become more aggressive once it's recognised that people or other dogs are afraid of it. If you try to correct this behaviour, you first have to try to understand what the dog is afraid of. Professional advice is a good idea here, as the wrong approach can easily make the problem worse.

The dominant-aggressive dog's body language is different. Its ears are pricked and its tail is raised and stiff. This dog will go only for its victim's arms, legs or throat. It is self-assured and highly placed in the dog hierarchy. Its attack is a display of power rather than a consequence of fear. This dog needs to know who's boss. You must bring it up rigorously and with a strong hand. An obedience course can help.

A dog may also show aggression when in pain. This is a natural defensive reaction. In this case try to resolve the dog's fear as far as possible. Reward it for letting you get to the painful spot. Be careful, because a dog in pain may also bite its master! Muzzling it can help prevent problems if you have to do something that may be painful. Never punish a dog for this type of aggression!

Socialisation

If your dog behaves in a timid manner, the reason for this behaviour can usually be found in the first few weeks of its life. A lack of new experiences in this very important so-called 'socialisation phase' has a big influence on the adult dog's behaviour. If a dog does not get to see humans, other dogs or other animals during this phase, it will be distant later. This distance is common with dogs that have grown up in a barn or kennel, with very little human contact. As mentioned above, fear can lead to aggression. It is very important that the dog gets as many new experiences as possible during its first few weeks. Take it into town in the car or on the bus, walk down a busy street with it and let it have a lot of contact with people, other dogs and other animals.

It's a huge task to turn an anxious, poorly socialised dog into a real pet. It will probably take an enormous amount of attention, love, patience and energy to get such an animal used to everything around it. Reward it often and give it plenty of time to adapt and, over time, it will learn to trust you and become less anxious. Try not to force anything, because that will always have the reverse effect. Here too, an obedience course can help a lot.

Dogs are often frightened of strangers. Have visitors give it something tasty as a treat. Put a can of dog biscuits by the door, so that your visitors can spoil your dog when they arrive. Here again, don't try to force anything. If the dog is still frightened, leave it in peace.

Dogs are often frightened in certain situations; well-known examples are thunderstorms and fireworks. In these cases try to ignore your dog's anxious behaviour. If you react to its whimpering and whining, it's the same as rewarding it. If you ignore its fear completely, the dog will quickly learn that nothing is wrong. You can speed up this 'learning process' by rewarding its positive behaviour.

Rewarding

Rewarding forms the basis for bringing up a dog. Rewarding good behaviour works far better than punishing bad behaviour and rewarding is also much more fun. Over time the opinions on how to bring up dogs have gradually changed. In the past, a sharp pull on the lead was considered the appropriate way to correct bad behaviour. Today, experts view rewards as a

positive incentive to get dogs to do what we expect of them.

There are many ways of rewarding a dog. The usual ways are a stroke or a friendly word, even without a tasty treat to go with it. When bringing up a puppy, a tasty treat at the right moment will do wonders, though. Make sure that you always have something tasty in your pocket to reward it for good behaviour.

Another form of reward is play. Whenever a dog notices that you have a ball in your pocket, it won't go far from your side. As soon as you've finished playing, put the ball away. This way your dog will always do its best in exchange for a game.

Despite the emphasis you put on rewarding good behaviour, a dog can sometimes be a nuisance or disobedient. You must correct such behaviour immediately. Always be consistent: once 'no' must always be 'no'.

Barking

Dogs that bark too much and too often are a nuisance for their surroundings. A dog-owner may tolerate barking up to a point, but neighbours are often annoyed by the unnecessary noise. Don't encourage your puppy to bark and yelp. Of course, it should be able to announce its presence, but if it goes on barking it must be called

to order with a strict 'Quiet!'. If your puppy does not listen, you can gently hold its muzzle closed with your hand.

A dog will sometimes bark for long periods when left alone. It feels threatened and tries to get someone's attention by barking. There are special training programmes for this problem, where a dog learns that being alone is nothing to be afraid of, and that its master will always return.

You can practise this with your dog at home. Leave the room and come back in at once. Reward your dog if it stays quiet. Gradually increase the length of your absences and keep rewarding it as long as it remains quiet. Never punish your dog if it does bark or yelp. It will never understand punishment afterwards, and this will only make the problem worse. Never go back into the room as long as your dog is barking, as it will view this as a reward.

You might want to make the dog feel more comfortable by switching the radio on for company during your absence. It will eventually learn that you always come back and the barking will reduce. If you don't get the required result, attend an obedience course.

Reproduction

Dogs, and thus also Yorkies and Silkies, follow their instincts, and reproduction is one of nature's most important processes. For people who enjoy breeding dogs this is a positive circumstance.

Those who simply want a 'cosy companion' however, will miss the regular adventures with females on heat and unrestrainable males like a toothache. But knowing a little about reproduction in dogs will help you to understand why they behave the way they do, and what measures you need to take when this happens.

Liability

Breeding dogs is much more than simply 1+1= many. If you're planning to breed with your terrier, be on your guard. The whole affair can quite easily turn into a financial disaster, because, under the law, a breeder is liable for the 'quality' of his puppies.

The kennel clubs place strict conditions on animals used for breeding. They need to be tested for certain hereditary abnormalities (see the chapter Your dog's health). By doing this, a breeder shows that he cares. If you breed a litter of puppies and sell them without having had these tests done, you can be held liable by the new owners for any costs arising from any inherited defects. These (veterinary) costs can be enormous! So contact a breeder club if you plan to breed a litter of puppies.

The female in season

Bitches become sexually mature at about eight to twelve months. Then they go into season for the first time. They are 'on heat' for two to three weeks. During this period they discharge little drops of blood and they are very attractive to males. The bitch is fertile during the second half of her season, and will accept a male to mate. The best time for mating is then between the ninth and thirteenth day of her season. A female's first season is often shorter and less severe than those that follow. If you do want to breed with your bitch, you must allow the first and the second season to pass. Most bitches go into season twice per year.

If you do plan to breed with your terrier in the future, then sterilisation is not an option to prevent unwanted offspring. A temporary solution is a contraceptive injection, although this is controversial because of side effects such as womb infections.

Phantom pregnancy

A phantom pregnancy is a not uncommon occurrence. The female behaves as if she has a litter. She takes all kinds of things to her basket and treats them like puppies. Her milk teats swell and sometimes milk is actually produced. The female will sometimes behave aggressively towards people or other animals, as if she is defending her young.

Phantom pregnancies usually begin two months after a season and can last a number of weeks.

If it happens to a bitch once, it will often re-occur after every season. If she suffers under it, sterilisation is the best solution, because continual phantom pregnancies increase the risk of womb or teat conditions. A sterilisation can, however, influence the coat structure, which will make the hair prone to becoming tangled more easily.

In the short term a hormone treatment is worth trying, perhaps also homeopathic medicines. Camphor spirit can give relief when teats are heavily swollen, but rubbing the teats with ice or a cold cloth (moisten and freeze) can also help relieve the pain. Feed the female less than usual, and make sure she gets enough distraction and extra exercise.

Preparing to breed

If you do plan to breed a litter of puppies, you must first wait for your female to be physically and mentally full-grown. In any event you must wait until her third season. To mate a bitch, you need a male. You could simply let her out on the street and she would quickly return home pregnant. But if you have a purebred Yorkie or Silky, then it certainly makes sense to mate her with the best possible candidate, even if she does not have a pedigree. Be meticulous with your preparations. Think especially about the following:

Accompanying a bitch through pregnancy, birth and the first eight to twelve weeks afterwards is a time-consuming affair. Never breed with dogs that have congenital defects, and the same applies to dogs without papers! The same goes for hyperactive, nervous and shy dogs.

If your dog does have a pedigree, then mate her with a dog that also has one. For more information, contact the breed association. You will find the addresses in the chapter Breed Associations.

Pregnancy

It's often difficult to tell at first if a bitch is pregnant. Only after about four weeks can you feel the pups in her belly. She will now slowly become fatter and her behaviour will usually change. Her teats will swell during the last few weeks of pregnancy.

The average pregnancy lasts 63 days, and costs the bitch a lot of energy. In the beginning she is fed her normal amount of food, but her nutritional needs increase in jumps during the second half of the pregnancy. Give her approximately fifteen percent more food each week from the fifth week on. The mother-to-be needs extra energy and proteins during this phase of her pregnancy. During the last weeks you can give her a concentrated food, which is rich in energy,

such as dry puppy food. Divide this into several small portions per day, as she can no longer deal with large portions of food. Towards the end of the pregnancy, her energy needs can easily be one-and-a-half times more than usual.

After about seven weeks the mother will start to demonstrate nesting behaviour and to look for a place to give birth to her young. This might be her own basket or a special birthing box. This must be ready at least a week before the birth to give the mother time to get used to it. The basket or box should preferably be in a quiet place.

The birth

The average litter counts three to five puppies. The birth normally takes place without too many problems. If you are in any doubt, you must contact your vet straight away, of course!

Birth

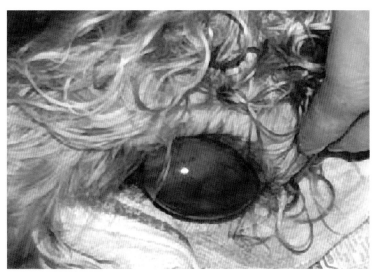

Yorkshire terrier puppies are born with smooth hair. They are black with some rust-brown (tan) markings. The colour changes at the age of approximately three to six months, but it can be as late as twelve to eighteen months. At the age of two to three years, the coat will have its final colour. The colour change starts on the head, which lightens up to a slate-blue and finally gets its end-colour. If your puppies are the right colour too early, they will probably become too light over time. Silky terriers are born completely black and with smooth hair. In the case of the Silky, too, the colour changes progressively.

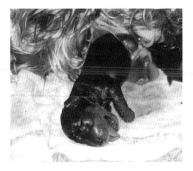

Suckling and weaning

After giving birth, the mother starts to produce milk. The suckling period is very demanding. During the first three to four weeks the pups rely entirely on their mother's milk. During this time she needs extra food and fluids. This can be up to three or four times the normal amount. If she's producing too little milk, you can give both the mother and her young special puppy milk.

Here too, divide the high quantity of food the mother needs into several smaller portions. Again, choose a concentrated, high-energy, food and give her plenty of fresh drinking water. Do not give the bitch cow's milk, as this can cause diarrhoea.

You can give the puppies some supplemental solid food when they are three to four weeks old. There are special puppy foods available that follow on well from the mother's milk and can easily be eaten with their milk teeth.

Ideally, the puppies are fully weaned at an age of six or seven weeks, i.e. they no longer drink their mother's milk. The mother's milk production gradually stops and her food needs also drop. Within a few weeks after weaning, the mother should be back to getting the same amount of food as before the pregnancy.

Castration and sterilisation

As soon as you are sure that your bitch should never bear a (new) litter, a vasectomy or sterilisation is the best solution. During sterilisation (in fact this is normal castration) the uterus and the ovaries are removed in an operation. The bitch no longer goes into season and can never become pregnant. The best age for a sterilisation is about eighteen months, when the bitch is more or less fully grown.

A male dog is usually only castrated for medical reasons or to correct undesirable sexual behaviour. During a castration the testicles are removed, which is a simple procedure and usually without complications. There is no special age for castration but, where possible, wait until the dog is fully grown. Vasectomy is sufficient where it's only a case of making the dog infertile. In this case the dog keeps its sexual drive but can no longer reproduce.

Of course, castration and sterilisation change the hormone levels. This can even influence the coat structure. In the case of some breeds, the hairs lose their outer layer, which makes them shine, and they become totally dry and dull. The coat might tangle up more easily and can even become totally matted. Before deciding to have your dog sterilised or castrated, get plenty of information from your vet.

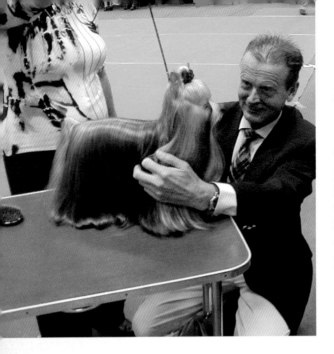

Shows

Visiting a dog show is a pleasant experience for both dog and master, and for some dog-lovers it has become a hobby. They visit countless shows every year.

Being judged

Others find it nice to visit an exemption show with their dog just once. It's worth making the effort to visit an exemption show where a judge's experienced eyes will inspect your terrier and assess it for form, condition and behaviour. The judge's report will teach you your dog's weak and strong points, which may help you when choosing a mate for breeding. You can also exchange experiences with other Yorkie or Silky owners. Official shows are only open to dogs with pedigrees.

Ring training

If you've never been to an exemption show, you're probably tapping in the dark in terms of what will be expected of you and your dog. Many kennel clubs organise so-called ring training courses for dogs going to an exemption show

for the first time. This training teaches you exactly what the judge will be looking for, and you can practise the correct techniques together with your dog.

Club matches

Almost all kennel clubs organise club matches. You have to enter your dog in a certain class before the big day. These meetings are usually small and friendly and are often the first acquaintance dog and master make with a judge. This is an overwhelming experience for your dog - a lot of its contemporaries and a strange man or woman who fiddles around with it and peers into its mouth. After a few times, your dog will know exactly what's expected of it and will happily go to the next club match.

Championship shows

Various championship shows take place during the course of the year, offering different prizes. These shows are much more strictly organised than club matches. Here, too, your dog must be registered in a certain class in advance and it will then be listed in a catalogue. On the day itself, the dog is kept in a cage (indoor kennel) until its turn comes up. During the judging in the ring, it's important that you show your dog at its best. The judge will give an official verdict and write a report. When all the dogs from that class have been judged, the winner is selected. You can pick up your report, and possibly your prize, after the class has finished.

The winners of the various classes will then compete for the title of Best of Breed. A winner will be chosen from the dogs belonging to the same breed group. The various winners of the different breed groups will then compete for Best in Show.

Do not forget!

If you want to visit a show with your dog, you need to be well prepared. You must certainly not forget the following:

For yourself:
• Registration card
• Food and drink
• Safety pin for the catalogue number
• Chair(s)

For your dog:
• Food and drink bowls and food
• Dog blanket and perhaps a cushion
• Show lead
• A brush
• Some chalk to clean its coat

If you have any more questions about dog shows, you can contact your local breed association or kennel club.

Getting ready for a show

Of course, your dog needs to be in perfect condition for a show. The judge will not be impressed if your dog's coat is dirty or tangled or if its paws are muddy. To start with, let an experienced dog groom or breeder show you how to get your dog ready for a show. Especially with the long coats of Yorkies and Silkies, it is very important to do this properly. You can quite easily 'mess things up' with your dog's coat, and it takes quite a while for it to grow back to full length. The nails must be cut properly and the teeth need to be free of tartar. Your dog must not be suffering from any parasites or diseases. A bitch must not be in season and a dog must be in possession of both testicles. Judges also don't like dogs that are badly brought up, timid or nervous.

Parasites

All dogs are vulnerable to various sorts of parasites. Parasites are tiny creatures that live at the expense of another animal. They feed on blood, skin and other body substances.

There are two main types. Internal parasites live within their host animal's body (tapeworm and roundworm) and external parasites live on the animal's exterior, usually in its coat (fleas and ticks), but also in its ears (ear mite).

Fleas

Fleas feed on a dog's blood. They cause not only itching and skin problems, but can also carry infections such as tapeworm. In large numbers they can cause anaemia and dogs can also become allergic to a flea's saliva, which can cause serious skin conditions.

So it's important that you treat your dog for fleas as effectively as possible. Do not just treat the animal itself, but also its surroundings. For treating your dog, there are various medicines: drops for the neck and to put in its food, flea collars, long-life sprays and flea powders. There are various sprays in pet shops, which can be used to eradicate fleas in the dog's immediate surroundings. Choose a spray that kills both adult fleas and their larvae. If your dog goes in your car, you should spray that too.

Fleas can also affect other pets, so you should treat those too. When spraying a room, cover any aquarium or fishbowl. If the spray reaches the water, it can be fatal for your fish! Your vet and pet shop have a wide range of flea treatments and can advise you on the subject.

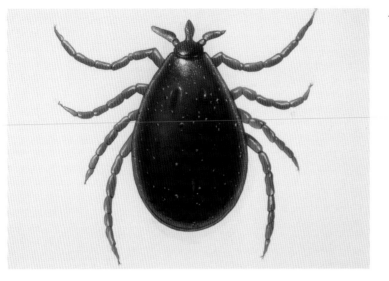

Tick

Ticks

Ticks are small, spider-like parasites. They feed on the blood of the animal or person they've settled on. A tick looks like a tiny, grey-coloured leather bag with eight feet. When it has sucked itself full, it is darker in colour and can easily be five to ten times its own size.

Dogs usually fall victim to ticks in bushes, woods or long grass. Ticks cause not only irritation by their blood-sucking, but can also carry a number of serious diseases. This applies especially to the Mediterranean countries, which can be infested with blood parasites. In our country these diseases are fortunately less common. But Lyme disease, which can also affect humans, has reached our shores. Your vet can prescribe a special treatment if you're planning to take your dog to southern Europe. It is important to fight ticks as effectively as possible. Check your dog regularly, especially when it's been running free in woods and bushes. It can also wear an anti-tick collar.

Removing a tick is simple using a tick pincette. Grip the tick with the pincette, as close to the dog's skin as possible, and carefully pull it out. You can also grip the tick between your fingers and, using a turning movement, pull it carefully out. You must disinfect the spot where the tick was, using iodine to prevent infection. Never soak the tick in alcohol, ether or oil. In a shock reaction the tick may discharge the infected contents of its stomach into the dog's skin.

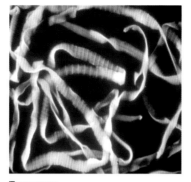

Tapeworm

Roundworm

Worms

Dogs can suffer from various types of worm. The most common are tapeworm and roundworm. Tapeworm causes diarrhoea and poor condition. With a tapeworm infection you can sometimes find small pieces of the worm around the dog's anus or on its bed. In this case, the dog must be wormed. You should also check your dog for fleas, as these can carry the tapeworm infection.

Roundworm is a condition that reoccurs regularly. Puppies are often infected by their mother's milk. Roundworm causes problems (particularly in younger dogs), such as diarrhoea, loss of weight and stagnated growth. In serious cases the pup becomes thin, but with a swollen belly. It may vomit and you can then see the worms in its vomit. They are spaghetti-like tendrils. In its first year, a puppy needs to be treated every three months with a worm treatment. Adult dogs should be treated every six months.

Your Yorkie' or Silky's health

We will give you some information about illnesses and abnormalities which are more common to the Yorkshire Terrier than to other breeds.

Patella luxation

In the case of this abnormality, the kneecap is not placed centrally at the end of the shinbone. The kneecap ends up next to the joint. A luxating kneecap can occur if the groove is not deep enough. This can be hereditary, but it can also be the result of trauma (an accident). In this case the luxation will be combined with ruptured ligaments. Luxation occurs in different severities. The amount of pain and discomfort varies per dog. Luxating kneecaps cannot be corrected surgically. Slippery floors and strange movements (such as running after balls too wildly, bouncing and quick turns) are not healthy for the joints of any dogs, whether they are big or small, puppies or adults.

Progressive Retina Atrophy (PRA)

PRA is a degenerative condition of the retina and will eventually result in blindness. In the beginning, the dog will have full sight in the daylight until it is approximately five years old. It will become totally blind between five and nine years of age.

Cataracts

Dogs are examined for cataracts (or Grey Star) at the same time as for PRA. This condition is caused by a clouding of the retina. It can occur at a young age and it is passed on by both parent animals. If only part of the retina is affected, cataracts need not lead to total blindness. Unfortunately, they usually do, however.

Entropion and ectropion

These are hereditary conditions of the eyelids. In the case of entropion, the eyelid curls to the inside, in the case of ectropion to the outside. The eyelashes will come in contact with the eyeball, which will result in irritation and red watering eyes. The eyes will become inflamed and discharge pus. This can lead to serious damage to the cornea and eventually to blindness. Entropion and ectropion can be corrected surgically.

Tips for terriers

- Buy your Yorkshire terrier or Australian Silky terrier via a breed association.
- Try to visit several breeders before buying a puppy.
- Its first trip in the car is very exciting for a puppy. Try to make it a pleasant experience.
- Yorkies and Silkies are lively dogs, but they cannot stand a hard hand.
- Yorkies and Silkies can be quite stubborn, so be consistent in their upbringing.
- Attend a puppy course with your dog. It teaches both dog and owner a lot.
- Ignore timid or submissive behaviour and don't be tempted to comfort your dog.
- Give plenty of attention to your dog's silky coat every day.

- Don't fight just fleas, but also their larvae.
- Hard dry food and plenty of dog chews help to keep your dog's teeth healthy.
- Never buy a puppy whose mother you weren't able to see.
- Make sure that your dog doesn't become too fat. Not too much food and plenty of exercise are the golden rules.

Breed Associations

You never know if you ever need advice or more information. Perhaps you take an interest in showing your dog. An address of a nearby breed association is always good to have around.

Being a member of a breed association gives you background information about your dog. You receive a club magazine. Club members come together for meetings and lectures organised by your club.
When becoming a member you are always up to date about developments of your breed. After all, who would miss an evening about grooming a Yorkshire terrier? Feel free to contact any of these associations:

Cheshire & North Wales Yorkshire Terrier Society
Secretary: Mrs J Milner
Tel: 0151 3272276

Midland Yorkshire Terrier Club
Secretary: Mrs S Graham
Tel: 01452 611282

Eastern Counties Yorkshire Terrier Club
Secretary: Mrs Pooley
For further information contact the Kennel Club

Lincoln & Humberside Yorkshire Terrier Club
Secretary: Mrs Walker
Tel: 01765 602265

Northern Counties Yorkshire Terrier Club
Secretary: Ms Watson
Tel: 01226 781373

South Western Yorkshire Terrier Club
Secretary: Mrs J Drake
Tel: 0117 9601592

Ulster Yorkshire Terrier Club
Secretary: Mr S. Larkham
Tel: 02893 378302

Yorkshire Terrier Club
Secretary: Mrs P E Mitchell
Tel: 01235 833171

Yorkshire Terrier Club of South Wales
Secretary: Mr T M Evans
Tel: 01443 431052

Yorkshire Terrier Club of Scotland
Secretary: Ms Burns
Tel: 01592 759277

The Yorkshire terrier

FCI classification:	Terriers, group 86, section 4
Country of origin:	Great Britain
Original task:	Hunting rats
Present task:	Companion and show dog
Character:	Lively, loyal, inquisitive, obedient
Colour:	Steel-blue with tan
Particular needs:	Intensive daily coat care
Height at shoulders:	Approximately 23 cm
Weight:	2.5 tot 3.5 kg
Life expectancy:	12 to 15 years

Australian Silky terrier

FCI classification:	Terriers, group 236, section 4
Country of origin:	Australia
Original task:	Companion and show dog
Character:	Assertive, lively, affectionate and clever
Colour:	Blue and tan or grey-blue and tan
Particular needs:	Intensive daily coat care
Height at shoulders:	Approximately 23 cm, bitches a little smaller
Weight:	3.5 to 4.5 kg
Life expectancy:	12 to 15 years

the **Yorkshire Terrier**